ART OF MINISTRY

The Impact of Time, Talent, and Treasure in the Ministry

ELLIOT LUABEYA

COPYRIGHT & PERMISSIONS

The Bible quotations used in this book are taken from the following Bible versions:

*New King James (**NKJV**)*
*Amplify Bible (**AMP**)*
*New Living Translation (**NLT**)*
*New International Version (**NIV**)*

Contact

E-mail/elliotluabeya15000@gmail.com
Phone: +233557559205
Facebook: Elliot LUABEYA
Tweeter: Elliot LUABEYA
Instagram: Elliot LUABEYA

Published by Fresh Word publishing
Phone +233552348265 / Mail: freshwordp@gmail.com

TABLES OF CONTENTS

DEDICATION

I humbly dedicate this book to my pastor and mentor **Reverend Guy BOMBOKO** for his unwavering assistance, counseling, teaching, love and patience throughout his coaching in the work of ministry. Your input has been a valuable asset in my ministry.

May the Lord remember and bless your endless sacrifices.

FOREWORD

Welcome to "The Art of Ministry: The Impact of Time, Talent, and Treasure."

As you embark on this journey through the pages of Pastor Elliot's insightful book, prepare to be equipped for the noble calling of ministry.

In these profound verses from Ephesians 4, we discover the divine orchestration of roles within the Body of Christ: apostles, prophets, evangelists, pastors, and teachers. Each bestowed with a unique gift, each entrusted with a sacred task to equip the saints for the work of ministry.

Pastor Elliot illuminates the truth that ministry is indeed an art form, one that can be learned and mastered. Through diligent study and application, we uncover the keys to effectiveness in serving God's kingdom.

Central to this artistry is the stewardship of time, talent, and treasure. Time, the precious currency of life, must be invested wisely in prayer, preaching, and the pursuit of God's purposes. Without a vision, time slips away unnoticed; but with vision, time becomes a cherished asset, redeemed for eternal significance.

Likewise, we are reminded of the God-given talents inherent within each of us. Yet, it is through refinement and dedication that these talents are honed to their fullest potential, enabling us to serve with excellence and impact.

And let us not overlook the importance of treasure the financial resources entrusted to our care. Effective stewardship of God's provision is paramount, for it is through faithful management that ministries flourish and God's kingdom advances.

Ultimately, our allocation of time, utilization of talent, and management of treasure reflect the depth of our love for God. As we offer our best — our hearts, souls, and strength — we demonstrate our commitment to His kingdom and His glory.

Within these pages, Pastor Elliot unveils the principles of effective stewardship, guiding us from mediocrity to fruitfulness in our divine calling.

Prepare to be transformed, to journey from glory to glory, as you embrace "The Art of Ministry."

May this book ignite a passion within you, propelling your ministry to new heights in the name of Jesus.

Blessings.

Your brother in the Lord.
Michel KIMI
Head Pastor of Gates of Zion
Community (Accra Ghana)

INTRODUCTION

In a world where spirituality and faith intersect with the complexities of human existence, beyond ritual and routine, ministry is an art form that blends dedication, compassion and leadership into a symphony of grace. The Art of Ministry is an invitation to explore the transformative power of heartfelt connections rooted in faith and compassion. Within its pages you will find profound insights, practical strategies and personal stories that illuminate the path to create soulful connections in a fragmented world, enabling you to become an instrument of love and healing in your ministry.

We speak of ministry as an art because it is something that we can learn or develop in order to be effective in our tasks. You cannot carry out your ministry successfully without having a particular knowledge in a particular area. This view encourages ministers to use their strengths, perspectives and personalities in carrying out their ministry.

If you are in the communications field, this aspect requires effective rhetoric, boldness and the ability to communicate complex concepts in a way that resonates with others. You need to be skilful and creative to inspire, challenge, comfort or enlighten your audiences. Being effective in ministry often requires good personalities, perspectives and practical experience to develop personal expression and authenticity.

It's safe to say that there are levels of service that involve improvisation and adapting to the needs and circumstances of the people we are serving.

If we go back to the Bible, we will find that the perfecting and equipping of the saints is also part of the work of the ministry that leads to the building up of the body of Christ; in maturity, truth and love.

> *For the equipping of the saints for the work of ministry, for the edifying of the body of Christ, till we all come to the unity of the faith and of the knowledge of the Son of God, to a perfect man, to the measure of the stature of the fullness of Christ;*
>
> **Ephesians 4:12-13**

So anyone who is involved in the work of ministry must know that it is our duty in this mission to learn more so that we can teach others.

> *And the things that you have heard from me among many witnesses, commit these to faithful men who will be able to teach others also.*
>
> **2 Timothy 2:2**

So it is our responsibility to raise up leaders, because since the time of

Christ there has been an endless chain of Christian discipleship.

The chapters of this book are designed in a simple way, to give us a clear picture of the ministry. Throughout the pages of this book we will be handling powerful subjects such as: Understanding the ministry; The Value of Time in Ministry; Nurturing and Utilizing Talent; Stewardship of Treasure in Ministry; Overcoming Barriers and Challenges; and Sustaining a Lifestyle of Ministry.

We pray that the Lord may guide us through the reading of this book and grant us wisdom to understand His mind and plan in this book.

SO LET READ AND BE BLESSED.

Chapter 1

UNDERSTANDING THE MINISTRY

The Bible does not explicitly provide a single, comprehensive definition of ministry. However, it does offer several principles and examples that can help shape our understanding of ministry. By definition, ministry is fundamentally about serving others. Ministry refers to the range of activities and services performed by believers to serve God and others. It includes various roles and functions such as preaching, teaching, counselling, evangelism, ministering to the needy, and many others.

As Christians in ministry, our goal is to spread God's love, help people grow spiritually, contribute positively to the community and impact the world with the Gospel message, following the example of Jesus Christ.

Jesus set the ultimate example of ministry by serving humanity through His teachings, miracles, and sacrificial death.

> *For even the Son of Man did not come to be served, but to serve, and to give his life as a ransom for many.*
>
> **Mark 10:45**

In the kingdom of God, whoever is first takes the lead in serving others. So Jesus, as the Son of God, His principle of leadership is self-giving service as He gives His life as a ransom. Christ, as our Saviour, laid down His sinless life so that sinful people must be saved; He was chosen and qualified to be the Saviour of the world. By His humiliating death and resurrection, our salvation was guaranteed. And it is in the light of these realities that Paul speaks of Christ as "our great God and Saviour".

#1 Biblical foundations of ministry

At the heart of the foundation of a ministry are the principles of love, service and discipleship. This foundation is built on the commands to love God with all our being and to love our neighbours as ourselves. Jesus' commission to make disciples of all nations, embracing people from diverse backgrounds and walks of life, the act of baptism and the act of teaching represent the ministry's commitment to fostering spiritual growth and leading individuals to a deeper understanding of faith. This directive from Jesus underscores the ministry's responsibility to spread the message of hope, compassion and salvation to all corners of the world.

The ministry is also called to show compassion by caring for those in need, such as orphans and widows. To do justice, love mercy and walk humbly with God embodies the ethos of humility, justice and compassion that defines the character of the ministry. These qualities not only shape its interactions with the world, but also guide its internal workings, fostering an environment of unity and shared purpose. This collective effort demonstrates the ministry's commitment to faith-filled service and exemplifies its role in creating a better world.

> *Jesus said to him, "'You shall love the LORD your God with all your heart, with all your soul, and with all your mind.' "This is the first and great commandment. "And the second is like it: 'You shall love your neighbour as yourself.'*
> **Matthew 22:37-39**

Go therefore and make disciples of all the nations, baptizing them in the name of the Father and of the Son and of the Holy Spirit, "teaching them to observe all things that I have commanded you; and lo, I am with you always, even to the end of the age." Amen.

Matthew 28:19-20

Pure and undefiled religion before God and the Father is this: to visit orphans and widows in their trouble, and to keep oneself unspotted from the world.

James 1:27

#2 Different forms of ministry

There are many different types of ministries listed in the Bible. Some of these ministries are mentioned in the Old Testament, while others are mentioned in the New Testament. Each of these ministries has a specific role to play in the Body of Christ. It is very important to understand the difference between these ministries because it will help us to discover our mission and also to understand God's plan for His people.

> *And He Himself gave some to be apostles, some prophets, some evangelists, and some pastors and teachers, for the equipping of the saints for the work of ministry, for the edifying of the body of Christ, till we all come to the unity of the faith and of the knowledge of the Son of God, to a perfect man, to the measure of the stature of the fullness of Christ;*

Ephesians 4:11-13

The apostle Paul lists some of the spiritual gifts given for leadership in the church. Apostles and prophets are mentioned as those who lay the foundation for God's church. The evangelist travels, taking the message of the gospel of Christ to places where it has not yet reached. Pastors and teachers work in local congregations.

This cluster of five gifts is often referred to as the five-fold ministry of the church. It is basic and fundamental to the planting and growth of the church. All other gifts are supportive. Spiritual gifts are given to church leaders for the specific purpose of equipping other believers for works of service that will build up the church to maturity and perfection in Christ. Thus, spiritual gifts are not given for the benefit of the leaders, but are to be used to help the church grow physically and spiritually until it reaches maturity. Here are brief lists of the five-fold ministry:

1. **Apostles:** The term apostle, meaning "messengers" or "ambassadors", in its strictest sense refers to those who saw

Christ in resurrected form and were specially chosen by Christ to tell others about Him from their eyewitness accounts. In the early Church, apostles were those sent out with a specific mission or purpose. They played a vital role in spreading the gospel and planting new churches.

PAUL, an apostle (not from men nor through man, but through Jesus Christ and God the Father who araised Him from the dead),

Galatians 1:1

2. **Prophets:** Are people called to deliver direct revelations from God. They foretold God's future actions and proclaimed what God had already said in the Scriptures to the Church for its edification, exhortation and encouragement.

Surely the Lord GOD does nothing, unless He reveals His secret to His servants the prophets.

Amos 3:7

3. **Evangelists:** They are people who have a special gift for sharing the good news of Jesus Christ with others. They have a passion for evangelism and are often involved in activities such as preaching, personal witnessing and organising outreach programmes.

But you be watchful in all things, endure afflictions, do the work of an evangelist, fulfil your ministry.

2 Timothy 4:5

4. **Pastors:** Also known as shepherds or overseers, they are responsible for the spiritual care and leadership of a local church. Their role is to guide, teach and nurture the members of the

church, providing pastoral support, counselling and spiritual guidance.

Shepherd the flock of God which is among you, serving as overseers, not by compulsion but willingly, not for dishonest gain but eagerly; nor as being lords over those entrusted to you, but being examples to the flock; and when the Chief Shepherd appears, you will receive the crown of glory that does not fade away.

1 Peter 5:2-4

5. **Teachers:** Are individuals who have a gift for effectively explaining and communicating biblical truths. They are skilled in the interpretation and application of Scripture, and their primary task is to instruct and train others in the knowledge and understanding of God's Word.

MY brethren, let not many of you become teachers, knowing that we shall receive a stricter judgment. For we all stumble in many things. If anyone does not stumble in word, he is a perfect man, able also to bridle the whole body.
James 3:1-2

In addition to the commonly recognised five-fold ministry, there are several other forms or types of ministry that exist within Christian leadership. These ministries can vary in focus and scope depending on the size, culture and specific needs of the church. It's important to recognise that each type of ministry plays a vital role in the holistic functioning of a church community and in carrying out the mission of sharing the Gospel. Here are some of them:

> ➢ **Worship ministry:** This involves facilitating and leading the congregation in worship during the service. Worship leaders, musicians and choir

leaders play an important role in creating a meaningful and engaging worship experience through music, singing and other forms of expression.

> **Prayer ministry:** Focuses on intercession and prayer for individuals, the church and various needs.

> **Counselling ministry:** To provide guidance, support and biblical counselling to those facing personal and relational challenges.

> **Children ministry:** Focus on the spiritual growth and education of children within the church community.

> **Youth ministry:** Working with young people to help them grow spiritually and meet the particular challenges they face.

> **Mission ministry:** Get involved in outreach and evangelism, both locally and globally.

And many more

The way to maturity is for all believers to be united in their faith and to have a common knowledge of the Son of God. To achieve this, leaders must nurture and protect the church and teach sound doctrine and faith. The ultimate goal is for all members and the church as a whole to become complete in Christ.

#3 Challenges and rewards of ministry

Spiritual attraction is often the primary motivator for most people who seek to enter Christian ministry. From responding to God's call, to training and guiding church members in spiritual growth contexts, to spreading the Word of God, pastors, ministers and other church leaders have awesome responsibilities.

As ministers step into different roles to meet these needs, they face great challenges along the way, but all for some of the greatest rewards a calling or career has to offer.

Most of the time, ministry involves facing spiritual and physical challenges and opposition; as God's servants, we must understand that there will always be a spiritual and physical battle between good and evil forces whenever we engage in sharing the message of the Gospel. We are exposed to criticism, rejection or even hostility from those who disagree with or oppose the faith.

Sometimes life may look unfair because as we all know pastors and church leaders have the responsibility in their holistic ministry to take care of the various needs of the believers even if they have made some mistakes the pastor will be there to form and help them out of that situation. But surprisingly, when believers hear that pastors or any church leaders have been accused of something even if it is not true; that tragedy will be exposed everywhere even on social media, they will be criticised, humiliated and abandoned. Forgetting that we are human and we need each other; when you were in trouble, he was there for you, but when he is in trouble, you have abandoned him.

As Christians, we need to cultivate the habit of praying for our pastors and church leaders. It's a way of offering support, guidance and strength to those who lead and serve the church. Like everyone else, pastors face challenges and struggles, and prayer is believed to provide spiritual encouragement and protection. It's also seen as a way of lifting them up and helping them to be effective in their role.

Keep praying for us, for we are convinced that we have a good conscience, seeking to conduct ourselves honourably [that is, with moral courage and personal integrity] in all things.

Hebrews 13:18 (Amplified)

Brothers and sisters, pray for us.
1 Thessalonians 5:25

We also need to understand that ministry is not only about pain and suffering; it is also about rewards. While ministry is often driven by a sense of calling and a desire to serve others, it can also bring personal fulfillment, spiritual growth and a deep sense of purpose. Building connections with a community, witnessing positive change in people's lives, and making a meaningful impact can be rewarding aspects of ministry. However, it's important to note that the rewards of service are not always material or tangible; they often come from a sense of contributing to something greater than oneself.

Serving the Lord by spreading the Gospel and caring for others can bring a deep sense of purpose and satisfaction. Seeing positive changes in the lives of the people you have helped, led and supported can bring incredible joy to your heart.

One of the benefits of ministry is that it helps us to build strong relationships within a community, fostering a sense of belonging and support. Leading a ministry for some time can challenge you to develop leadership, communication and interpersonal skills, leading to personal growth.

As Christians, we should never forget that those who serve with a sincere heart and dedication to God and others are believed to be rewarded in eternity for their faithful service.

> *His lord said to him, 'Well done, good and faithful servant; you were faithful over a few things, I will make you ruler over many things. Enter into the joy of your lord.*
>
> **Matthew 25:21**

Chapter 2

THE VALUE OF TIME IN MINISTRY

Every job in the world is designed to follow a specific time schedule in which workers must complete their tasks. And while you are working somewhere, you will be given the job description, which contains all the requirements for that job, as well as the opening and closing time. These requirements must be strictly adhered to by all workers, especially the time aspect. You cannot come to work whenever you want and leave whenever you want.

Imagine you work in a bank or any other company where the starting time is fixed at 8am and you show up at 10am. No matter what explanation you can give, you will be in serious trouble; you can be blamed, suspended or even fired for not showing up on time.

We can see that many people are willing to work beyond their requirements; they may even work extra hours just to meet their targets, also because they want to build and protect their careers. So they need to be very respectful and considerate of their bosses, otherwise they will lose that job.

It is amazing to see how people all over the world, believers and non-believers alike, dedicate themselves to follow the instructions of their bosses in order to achieve their goals. But how sad it is to see that if there is one place where people have no respect for time, especially Christians, it is in the work of God; most of the time we see Christians working in the banks and any other business respecting time but not showing the same example of respect for time when it comes to the work of God. They all have the same excuses, "I am so busy during the week..."

As children of God, it is important to note that respecting time in ministry is more valuable to us because it shows our love and respect for God in what we do. Coming to church early is a sign of respect for God, respecting time in church or any other ministry work shows that we value the work of God more than anything else on earth. We must stop making excuses for not coming to church early or not doing the work of God at the appointed time; rather, we should find a reason why we should always be able to do the work of God on time.

I remember my pastor used to tell us that we must always find reasons why we should do the work of God, instead of finding excuses why we should not do the work of God. When your mind is sharpened in the service of God, time will not be a problem for you.

Ministry is all about serving; we cannot become ministers without having the mind of a servant. We must serve God wholeheartedly with our time; putting Him first and at the centre of everything we do.

If we can respect our bosses because of the worldly jobs we do, we must show more respect to God than to them. Because from these people we only receive monthly salaries that cannot even cover all our expenses, but we give them more credit and respect. How much more should we be grateful to God who gives us the breath of life every day and has given us the guarantee of eternal life? Dearly beloved, we must love God more than anything on earth by giving Him what is precious, our time.

#1 Strategies for effective time management

In order to avoid or reduce stress, we need to learn some approaches that can help us understand how to manage our time in ministry. Applying these principles can help us to balance our time between our ministry responsibilities and our personal lives, while seeking to honour God in all that we do. Here are some principles for time management:

1. **Seek God's Guidance**

    It's very important to begin our day by seeking God's guidance through prayer and meditation. We need to rely on His wisdom to help us make effective decisions about how to spend our time. We also need to spend most of our time focusing on meaningful tasks that contribute to the purpose and impact of our ministry.

Trusting in God is a conscious dependence on Him, much like relying on a tree for support. The command to acknowledge Him means to observe Him and get to know Him in the process of living, for a better future in ministry.

Trust in the LORD with all your heart, And lean not on your own understanding; In all your ways acknowledge Him, And He shall direct your paths.

Proverbs 3:5-6

2. **Plan with Diligence**

Effective time management involves creating a well-structured plan for our ministry tasks; carefully allocating time for various responsibilities to avoid wasting precious moments.

Thoughtful planning by diligent individuals is compared to the imprudent haste of those who rush. Just as planning invariably leads to profit, undue haste inevitably leads to poverty.

The plans of the diligent lead surely to plenty, But those of everyone who is hasty, surely to poverty.

Proverbs 21:5

3. Avoid Busyness

It's necessary to learn how to balance our personal and ministry time. As Christians, we need to regularly schedule time for both personal activities and ministry responsibilities. We also need to communicate regularly with our church or ministry team to ensure that everyone is aware of our availability. And never forget that taking care of our own spiritual, emotional and physical well-being enables us to be more effective in our ministry.

Being busy doesn't mean that you are effective in what you do, because being busy usually means that someone is actively involved in the work of God, often as part of their role within the church or community. This can include tasks such as leading worship, teaching, counselling and other tasks related to the practical work of the church or community. Being too busy can affect the quality of our work in ministry and limit our ability to focus effectively on core tasks.

See then that you walk circumspectly, not as fools but as wise, redeeming the time, because the days are evil

Ephesians 5:15-16

4. Delegate and Equip

Don't try to do everything yourself; you need to delegate tasks to capable team members or volunteers and empower them to contribute to the work of the ministry.

Just as Jethro (Moses' father-in-law) advised Moses to delegate tasks to capable people, we need to recognise the value of delegating authority in ministry; and equipping others to share the same workload will allow us to focus on tasks that are in line with our strengths and calling. (**Exodus 18:17-23**)

And the things that you have heard from me among many witnesses, commit these to faithful men who will be able to teach others also.

2 Timothy 2:2

5. Avoid Procrastination

Procrastination is the act of delaying or postponing tasks, activities or responsibilities, especially those that are necessary or important. It involves putting off things that need to be done, often in favour of more immediate, less important or more enjoyable activities. It is a common behaviour that many people struggle with and can have negative consequences in various aspects of life and ministry, as it can hinder personal and professional productivity.

With the love of God in our hearts, we must give ourselves wholeheartedly to the work of ministry, whatever the time or circumstances.

I CHARGE you therefore before God and the Lord Jesus Christ, who will judge the living and the dead at His appearing and His kingdom: Preach the word! Be ready in season and out of season. Convince, rebuke, exhort, with all longsuffering and teaching.

2 Timothy 4:1-2

V5 *But you be watchful in all things, endure afflictions, do the work of an evangelist, fulfil your ministry.*

#2 Maximizing productivity in ministry

In order to be productive and maximise our impact in ministry, we need to define a clear and compelling mission statement for our ministry; we need to know the purpose and values that guide our work. Prioritise the core values and principles of our ministry and ensure that our actions are aligned with these values. Then identify the strengths and unique skills of our team members and assign roles that make the most of these strengths.

Here are some principles for maximizing our productivity and make impact in ministry:

1. **Prayer:** We need to prioritise prayer and spiritual growth within our team. A strong spiritual foundation can guide and sustain our ministry. God must be at the centre of everything we do in our lives and ministry.

All the ways of a man are pure in his own eyes, But the LORD weighs the spirits. Commit your works to the LORD, And your thoughts will be established.

Proverbs 16:2-3

2. **Innovate and Adapt:** Stay open to innovation and adapt to changing circumstances within the ministry. Be willing to try new approaches to achieve your ministry's goals.

Being open to innovation and change in the service is very important because it allows us to embrace new ideas that will help us maximise our productivity and effectiveness in our service.

3. **Adapt to Technology:** Embracing technology is helpful for good outreach, communication and management. We strongly encourage ministers to use social media platforms, websites and online tools to expand our mission and reach many people.

Making use of technology in ministry it one of the way to automate tasks, manage data, and also facilitate communication and visibility.

4. **Training and development:** Invest in ongoing training for your team members to improve their skills and productivity.

Everyone involved in ministry must learn to develop and build their skills and abilities. A trained person is a valuable weapon in the success of the ministry.

5. **Learn from Others:** Collaborating with other ministries, organisations and churches that share the same goals or vision can increase our impact in ministry.

Seeking advice and learning from experienced mentors or other successful ministries, can be seen as a key to unlocking our productivity. Their insights can be invaluable.

Productivity should be maximized while maintaining a healthy and ethical working environment. Remember that the impact of our ministry goes beyond numbers; it's about changing lives and bringing people closer to God.

Chapter 3

NURTURING AND UTILIZING TALENT

The idea of nurturing and using our talents for God's work is often rooted in various passages of Scripture. One of the key references can be found in the New Testament, specifically in the Gospel of Matthew, chapter 25, and verses 14-30, which includes the Parable of the Talents. Let's look at a brief summary of the parable:

In this parable, a master entrusts various sums of money (talents) to his servants before he goes on a journey. The servants who invest their talents wisely and make them grow are praised when the master returns, while the one who buries his talent is rebuked. The message here is that Christians are encouraged to use and multiply the abilities and resources God has given them for His purposes and not to waste them through fear or neglect.

After a long absence, the master returned to settle accounts. He asked each of his servants to account for what they had done with the money he had given them. The first two servants had to use the money to trade profitably, so they had put the talents to good use. These profitable servants were rewarded with greater responsibilities because they had the courage to take risks with the Lord's investment.

The third servant had misunderstood the nature of his responsibility. He took no risks in investing his talent; indeed, he was afraid to do so. He assumed that his role was to do nothing with the talent he was given, and he wasted the opportunity his master had given him. So his master took away the only talent he had and added it to the others who had used his investment wisely.

Allow me to tell you that God has richly blessed His people with His gifts. And these are not to be ignored or treated as ornaments for display. Instead, as individuals or as the body of Christ, we must see these gifts as investments to be used to bring glory to our Master. We must put faith into action by taking risks that will lead to fruitfulness.

#1 Explore the concept of talent as God-given abilities and gifts for ministry.

As Christians, we need to understand that the concept of talent refers to the God-given abilities and gifts that we possess, which are meant to be used for ministry and service to others. These talents can include a wide range of skills and qualities, such as teaching, leadership, compassion, creativity and more. Note that these talents are not random, but are purposely given by God to fulfill His divine plan and bring glory to Him.

So Christians are encouraged to discover, nurture and use their talents in various forms of ministry, whether it's in a church setting, community service or any area where they can make a positive impact and share God's love with others. It's seen as a way of honouring God and contributing to the betterment of the world.

Be hospitable to one another without grumbling. As each one has received a gift, minister it to one another, as good stewards of the manifold grace of God. If anyone speaks, let him speak as the oracles of God. If anyone ministers, let him do it as with the ability which God supplies, that in all things God may be glorified through Jesus Christ, to whom belong the glory and the dominion forever and ever. Amen.

1 Peter 4:9-11

We are called to offer hospitality to one another without complaint, because each of us has to use the gifts God has given us to help others. Whatever we have to say should be as if God Himself were speaking through us, and whenever we offer service, whether in our workplace or in the Church, it should be done wholeheartedly, making full use of the gifts God has given us.

So as we've explored this concept of talents as God-given abilities for the work of ministry, we've discovered that it's a process of self-discovery, development and service. Each of us needs to take time for self-reflection and prayer; to seek God's guidance in understanding our unique gifts and talents. We need to look at our interests, passions and skills to discover what we are naturally good at? What activities bring us joy and fulfilment? We are also free to consult with our church leaders, mentors or spiritual advisors. They can provide insight and guidance on how to discern our talents and where they might best be used in ministry.

> *God has given each of us the ability to do certain things well. So if God has given you the ability to prophesy, speak out when you have faith that God is speaking through you. If your gift is that of serving others, serve them well. If you are a teacher, do a good job of teaching. If your gift is to encourage others, do it! If you have money, share it generously. If God has given you leadership ability, take the responsibility seriously. And if you have a gift for showing kindness to others, do it gladly.*
>
> **Romans 12:6-8(NLT)**

We need to invest our time and effort in developing our talents, even if this means taking courses, attending workshops or practising regularly to improve our skills; we should get involved in different aspects of ministry in our churches or communities, trying out different roles to see where we feel most drawn and where our talents are best used.

Taking spiritual gift assessments or quizzes, often offered by churches or Christian organisations, can also be helpful in identifying our strengths and areas of gifting. Always be open to feedback from others, as sometimes those around us can see our gifts more clearly than we can.

Staying connected to our churches or fellowships for support and encouragement is the best way to grow in ministry. We must continually seek God's guidance through prayer, asking Him for wisdom and clarity in using our talents for His purposes.

Remember that ministry is about serving others in love, using our talents to meet the needs of others and bring them closer to God.

We should also understand that discovering and effectively using our talents for ministry is a lifelong journey of spiritual growth and service. It may take time to fully grasp how God wants us to serve Him. But as we continue to seek God's will and use our abilities to build His kingdom, we will find meaning and fulfilment in serving God and others.

#2 Help others to identify their unique talents and strengths.

Helping others to identify their unique talents and strengths is a way of encouraging them to use their God-given gifts for the betterment of the world and to fulfil their purpose in serving God. We are all created by God with skills and talents for a purpose.

By helping others to identify their strengths, we enable them to recognise and fulfil their God-given calling. Even the Bible teaches in 1 Peter 4:10 that we are stewards of the gifts and talents God has given us. Encouraging others to identify, develop and use their talents responsibly is a way of honouring this principle.

Within the Christian community, helping individuals discover their strengths contributes to the overall health and growth of the church. Each member has a unique role to play.

> *For as the body is one and has many members, but all the members of that one body, being many, are one body, so also is Christ. For by one Spirit we were all baptized into one body— whether Jews or Greeks, whether slaves or free—and have all been made to drink into one Spirit. For in fact the body is not one member but many.*

1 Corinthians 12:12-14

Here are some ways to help others identify their unique talents and strengths for ministry:

1. **Provide Support:** Provide mentorship, advice or guidance to help individuals explore their talents and passions.

   As iron sharpens iron, So a man sharpens the countenance of his friend.

   Proverbs 27:17

It's helpful to connect with experienced mentors or leaders in our churches who can provide guidance, accountability and wisdom to help us discover our gifts and move forward in our ministry journey.

2. **Lead by Example:** Demonstrate the use of your own gifts and talents for ministry and service as a model for others.

IMITATE me, just as I also imitate Christ.

1 Corinthians 11:1

And you became followers of us and of the Lord, having received the word in much affliction, with joy of the Holy Spirit, so that you became examples to all in Macedonia and Achaia who believe.

1 Thessalonians 1:6-7

When we lead by example, we don't just push our team members to excel, we actively demonstrate that excellence through our actions; good leadership is about using yourself as an example for your team members. Be what you want them to be.

3. **Embrace Challenges for your Growth:** You need to see challenges as opportunities for your growth and the refinement of your talents, trusting that God is with you. Also understand that developing your talents for effective ministry is a journey that may require patience and perseverance.

And not only that, but we also glory in tribulations, knowing that tribulation produces perseverance; and perseverance, character; and character, hope.

Romans 5:3-4

One of the best ways to learn how to identify your talents is to practice what you already know in order to develop other skills. We should never forget that God will always allow us to face challenges in our ministry to teach us perseverance and sharpen our character.

#3 Provide guidance on developing and honing these talents for impactful ministry

Developing and utilizing our talents for ministry can create a profound impact. Whether it's through teaching, community outreach, counseling, or any other talents we possess, nurturing these abilities with dedication and integrity can make a significant deference in the lives of others.

1. **Study and practice**

   Develop your skills through study and consistent practice, whether it's in theology, preaching, teaching, counselling or other areas of ministry.

Think of these trainings and internships as powerful tools for gaining practical experience.

Therefore I remind you to stir up the gift of God which is in you through the laying on of my hands. **2 Timothy 1:6**

2. Seek mentorship

Learning from experienced mentors or spiritual leaders in ministry can provide invaluable insight, wisdom, and guidance.

As Christians, we need to understand that people grow by interacting with each other.

The things which you learned and received and heard and saw in me, these do, and the God of peace will be with you.

Philippians 4:9

As iron sharpens iron, So a man sharpens the countenance of his friend.

Proverbs 27:17

3. Stay grounded in the Word of God

Study and meditate regularly on the Scriptures to understand

God's will and to align your talents with His purpose for your life. Cultivate your spiritual life through prayer, meditation, and the study of religious texts.

Everyone wants to be rich. Everybody wants to be successful. Here is the key to success provided by the Bible. Meditate on the Word of God by rehearsing it over and over in your mind to understand its implications for life's situations. The process of meditation leads to a change in thinking because God's thoughts can literally become our thoughts. Then we are more likely to do what God wants us to do. If we live in harmony with God's plan for our lives, we will be more successful and prosperous than if we ignore His teachings. A strong spiritual foundation is essential for effective ministry.

This Book of the Law shall not depart from your mouth, but you shall meditate in it day and night, that you may observe to do according to all that is written in it. For then you will make your way prosperous, and then you will have good success.

Joshua 1:8

#4 Ways to overcome challenges and limitations in using talent effectively

Overcoming challenges and limitations in using our talents requires maximum perseverance, adaptability and seeking support from community or mentors. It's about finding creative solutions, being open to change, nurturing resilience and staying true to your purpose and faith while overcoming obstacles.

Here are some practical ways to overcome the challenges and limitations of using talent effectively:

1. **Trust in God's plan**

    We must have faith in God because He has given us talents for a purpose and trust His guidance, He is in perfect control of everything we are dealing with.

God knows what He is doing and His plans for us will bring peace, not disaster. He is preparing a future full of hope for His people. Through challenges, God is preparing something fundamentally different and pleasant that will bring glory to His name.

For I know the thoughts that I think toward you, says the LORD, thoughts of peace and not of evil, to give you a future and a hope.

Jeremiah 29:11

2. **Facing Challenges**

    Obstacles must be seen as opportunities to grow and develop our talents; we must persevere in our pursuits despite challenges or failures.

Challenges are not pleasant and can be extremely painful, but as children of God we must see them as opportunities for rejoicing. Troubles and difficulties are an instrument that refines and purifies our faith, and produces patience and endurance.

My brethren, count it all joy when you fall into various trials, knowing that the testing of your faith produces patience. But let patience have its perfect work, that you may be perfect and complete, lacking nothing.

James 1:2-4

3. Perseverance

In ministry we may face rejection, conflict or slow progress, but perseverance helps us to remain steadfast in our mission despite these hurdles.

Many challenges may come our way to discourage us from expressing our talents, but we must not give up, because every challenge or limitation we face can be seen as an opportunity to learn something new and to deepen our faith and trust in the work of ministry.

Let us not become weary in doing good, for at the proper time we will reap a harvest if we do not give up.
Galatians 6:9 (NIV)

Chapter 4

STEWARDSHIP OF TREASURE IN MINISTRY

The concept of stewardship in ministry is about recognising that all resources ultimately belong to God. For example, Earthly treasures have a habit of disappointing their owners. They offer no lasting security. Clothes, even the most expensive, eventually wear out or are eaten by moths. Rust destroys metals, and there is always the risk of theft. Even money can deteriorate as a result of spiralling inflation.

That is why the Bible tells us to lay up treasures in heaven rather than on earth, emphasising the eternal value of investments in God's kingdom.

> *"Do not lay up for yourselves treasures on earth, where moth and rust destroy and where thieves break in and steal; "but lay up for yourselves treasures*

in heaven, where neither moth nor rust destroys and where thieves do not break in and steal. "For where your treasure is, there your heart will be also.

Matthew 6:19-21

But this I say: He who sows sparingly will also reap sparingly, and he who sows bountifully will also reap bountifully. So let each one give as he purposes in his heart, not grudgingly or of necessity; for God loves a cheerful giver. And God is able to make all grace abound toward you, that you, always having all sufficiency in all things, may have an abundance for every good work.

2 Corinthians 9:6-8

There is no better indicator of growth in the life of the ministry than in the area of giving. God is not primarily concerned with the amount of the gift, but with the motive behind it. The person who fails to honour God with his money is actually robbing God, not because he is impoverishing God, but because he is denying God's ordained means of supporting His work and His ministers.

To every child of God who honours God with his money, God promises abundant blessings and the provision of every need.

#1 The concept of stewardship in ministry

The concept of stewardship in ministry involves the responsible and faithful management of all resources entrusted to individuals or to a community. It involves recognizing that everything we have, whether talents or finances, is a gift from God.

Stewardship in ministry is a holistic approach that emphasizes the idea that believers are caretakers or stewards, not owners, of the church's resources. It's about using them wisely and for the greater good, in accordance with God's purposes and values. This concept is deeply rooted in various biblical teachings and encourages accountability, generosity and the ethical use of resources for the advancement of God's kingdom and the well-being of others.

> *Then God said, "Let Us make man in Our image, according to Our likeness; let them have dominion over the fish of the sea, over the birds of the air, and over the cattle, over all the earth and over every creeping thing that creeps on the earth."*
>
> **Genesis 1:26**

God sets the stage for stewardship by outlining humanity's role in caring for God's creation. He has established the idea that humans are to have dominion over the Earth, not as reckless rulers, but as responsible stewards.

And the Lord said, "Who then is that faithful and wise steward, whom his master will make ruler over his household, to give them their portion of food in due season? "Blessed is that servant whom his master will find so doing when he comes. "Truly, I say to you that he will make him ruler over all that he has.

Luke 12:42-44

This parable of the faithful steward highlights the importance of being found faithful in managing what has been given, and links this to the greater responsibility of overseeing the household in the absence of the master.

We need to recognize that finances are resources entrusted to us by God and therefore need to be managed with integrity, prudence and a focus on long-term impact rather than short-term gain. Stewardship in ministry is not just about financial management;

it's a way of life that involves managing all aspects of one's life as a sacred trust from God.

#2 Managing and allocating financial resources in ministry

The management and allocation of financial resources in the ministry is critical to ensuring that funds are used effectively for various activities such as outreach programs, community services, staffing, construction and other operational needs. Proper management helps to maintain transparency and accountability, and to achieve the goals of the ministry through the efficient use of available resources.

It involves a strategic and responsible approach to the use of funds in line with the organization's mission and values. It includes several key aspects:

1. **Budgeting**

   We have to develop a well-thought-out budget that reflects the ministry's goals and ensures that funds are allocated appropriately to various programs, operations, and outreach efforts.

For which of you, intending to build a tower, does not sit down first and count the cost, whether he has enough to finish it

Luke 14:28

2. **Transparency and Accountability**

   Maintain clear financial records and be accountable to donors and stakeholders. This includes regular financial reporting and transparent communication about how funds are used.

He who is faithful in what is least is faithful also in much; and he who is unjust in what is least is unjust also in much.

Luke 16:10

3. Prioritization

Allocate funding based on priorities, identifying critical needs and directing resources where they can have the greatest impact in line with the ministry's objectives.

The plans of the diligent lead surely to plenty, But those of everyone who is hasty, surely to poverty.

Proverbs 21:5

It is important to understand that managing and allocating financial resources in ministry requires a blend of financial insight, ethical considerations, and a deep understanding of the organization's mission to ensure that funds are used effectively to further the ministry's goals and serve the community.

#3 Fundraising and financial sustainability in ministry

Fundraising within a church organization involves raising financial support from members and sometimes the wider community to fund various activities, missions, projects or the running costs of the church. It includes events, campaigns or initiatives designed to raise funds or contributions and to foster a sense of community involvement and shared responsibility in supporting the church's initiatives or charitable causes. These efforts are designed to support and promote the mission, outreach and ministries of the church. Here are some supporting scriptures:

Honor the LORD with your possessions, And with the firstfruits of all your increase; So your barns will be filled with plenty, And your vats will overflow with new wine.

Proverbs 3:9-10

"Give, and it will be given to you: good measure, pressed down, shaken together, and running over will be put into your bosom. For with the same measure that you use, it will be measured back to you."

Luke 6:38

Pure and undefiled religion before God and the Father is this: to visit orphans and widows in their trouble, and to keep oneself unspotted from the world

James 1:27

But this I say: He who sows sparingly will also reap sparingly, and he who sows bountifully will also reap bountifully.

2 Corinthians 9:6

In the context of fundraising and financial sustainability, these verses are used to encourage us in the art of giving with a joyful heart; the principle of abundance that comes from faithful giving; and the focus on the spiritual aspect of giving rather than just the transaction itself.

We've come to understand that fundraising in a church or ministry is also a way for members to actively participate in the mission of the church, to contribute to the greater good, and to advance the kingdom of God.

In ministry, achieving financial sustainability through effective fundraising is critical to the continuity and growth of God's work.

> *The generous soul will be made rich, And he who waters will also be watered himself. The people will curse him who withholds grain, But blessing will be on the head of him who sells it.*
>
> **Proverbs 11:25-26**

#4 Ethical considerations in handling money and resources in ministry

The handling of money and resources in the church requires a high standard of ethical behaviour and stewardship. The Bible emphasises integrity and accountability in the management of finances.

Churches are entrusted with resources for the common good, which requires transparency, responsible budgeting and ethical decision-making. Maintaining honesty, avoiding conflicts of interest and ensuring that funds are used for their intended purpose honours God's principles and maintains the trust of the congregation and the community.

The integrity of the upright will guide them, But the perversity of the unfaithful will destroy them.
Proverbs 11:3

Here are some key ethical considerations along with supporting principles from scripture:

1. Honesty and Integrity

Are cornerstones of stewardship in ministry, advising us against dishonest gain and instead to work and share with those in need.

In ministry, prioritising transparency and maintaining integrity in the use of resources is not only consistent with Christian principles, but also builds trust, credibility and the ability to impact lives for the glory of God.

He who walks with integrity walks securely, But he who perverts his ways will become known.

Proverbs 10:9

2. Responsible Stewardship

It underlines the commitment to be wise stewards of the ministry's resources. Working with transparency and prudence ensures that resources are used effectively to fulfil the ministry's mission, honours God's purpose and fosters trust among believers and the community.

But he who did not know, yet committed things deserving of stripes, shall be beaten with few. For everyone to whom much is given, from him much will be required; and to whom much has been committed, of him they will ask the more.

Luke 12:48

3. Avoiding Misuse of Funds

This includes setting clear budgets, tracking expenses, auditing accounts regularly and educating members about how their contributions are being used. Implementing checks and balances is essential to ensure accountability and prevent potential mismanagement of funds.

For the love of money is a root of all kinds of evil, for which some have strayed from the faith in their greediness, and pierced themselves through with many sorrows.

1Timothy 9:10

Being a good steward of a church's finances is more than just a financial matter; it's about maintaining integrity and faithfulness. By embracing these principles and applying sound financial practices guided by biblical wisdom, trust, transparency and good stewardship can be cultivated.

This commitment ensures that funds are used wisely and serve the core principles of the church.

Chapter 5

OVERCOMING BARRIERS AND CHALLENGES

It is important to know that overcoming barriers and challenges in ministry is an essential aspect of doing God's work. It involves breaking problems down into smaller steps, seeking support when needed, and maintaining a positive attitude to finding solutions.

By overcoming these obstacles, ministries can better fulfil their purpose, connect with people, meet their needs and foster spiritual growth and unity. It's about adapting to serve effectively despite the challenges.

"Have I not commanded you? Be strong and of good courage; do not be afraid, nor be dismayed, for the LORD your God is with you wherever you go."

Joshua 1:9

#1 Common obstacles and challenges that individuals and communities face in leveraging time, talent, and treasure for ministry

Committing time, talent and treasure to ministry can be fraught with challenges, both at the individual and the church level. Here is a short list of common barriers:

1. **Time Constraints**

   Most people face time constraints due to personal commitments, work or family responsibilities. Balancing these with volunteer or service activities can be challenging. Prioritising and managing time effectively is crucial to overcoming this obstacle.

This means taking advantage of opportunities for service. We must use as much time as is possible for advancing Christ's purposes in this world.

See then that you walk circumspectly, not as fools but as wise, redeeming the time, because the days are evil
Ephesians 5:15-16

2. **Misalignment of Talents**

   Sometimes individuals may feel that their talents don't match the immediate needs of the ministry, leading to reluctance or under-utilisation of their skills. Fostering a culture that values diverse talents and finding creative ways to integrate different skills helps to address this challenge.

In ministry, the misalignment of talents can obscure effective ministry and impact. It can happen when someone's talents are not recognised or used effectively in ministry, leading to feelings of under-utilisation or dissatisfaction. We need to look to Scripture for guidance that can help us realign our talents in ministry to be useful and fulfil our spiritual calling.

Having then gifts differing according to the grace that is given to us, let us use them: if prophecy, let us prophesy in proportion to our faith; or ministry, let us use it in our ministering; he who teaches, in teaching; he who exhorts, in exhortation; he who gives, with liberality; he who leads, with diligence; he who shows mercy, with cheerfulness.

Romans 12:6-8

3. **Financial Limitations**

   Experiencing financial constraints can be a barrier to giving generously or providing adequate resources for ministry needs. Teaching the church about the impact of their contributions and fostering a culture of generosity can help overcome this barrier.

We need to teach the principles of stewardship and generosity, for God expects us to give freely from the blessings we receive.

Honor the LORD with your possessions, And with the firstfruits of all your increase.

Proverbs 3:9

By recognising and actively working to overcome these barriers, individuals and communities can make better use of their time, talents and treasure, and foster a more impactful and sustainable approach to ministry.

#2 Practical solutions, tips, and strategies for overcoming these barriers

Overcoming challenges and barriers in ministry often requires a combination of practical and spiritual approaches.

Here are some practical solutions that can help us overcome these situations:

1. Solutions for Time Constraints

To overcome time constraints, we need to encourage individuals to prioritise their service commitments by setting aside specific times for involvement. This will ensure that service activities are integrated into their daily routine. It is also important to distribute tasks among willing volunteers to share the workload. This not only reduces the workload, but also gets more people involved in the ministry.

This takes into account varying availability and encourages wider participation.

Listen now to my voice; I will give you counsel, and God will be with you: Stand before God for the people, so that you may bring the difficulties to God. And you shall teach them the statutes and the laws, and show them the way in which they must walk and the work they must do. Moreover you shall select from all the people able men, such as fear God, men of truth, hating covetousness; and place such over them to be rulers of thousands, rulers of hundreds, rulers of fifties, and rulers of tens. And let them judge the people at all times. Then it will be that every great matter they shall bring to you, but every small matter they themselves shall judge. So it will be easier for you, for they will bear the burden with you.

Exodus 18:19-22

2. Solution for Misalignment of Talents

As leaders, we need to conduct assessments to identify people's talents and interests and then match them to appropriate ministry needs, as well as multiply training or workshops to enhance skills that may be under-utilised but relevant to the ministry.

Encouraging continuous learning ensures that talents are aligned with evolving needs.

The heart of the prudent acquires knowledge, And the ear of the wise seeks knowledge. A man's gift makes room for him, And brings him before great men.

Proverbs 18:15-16

3. Solution for Financial Limitations

It is necessary to clearly communicate the impact of financial contributions on the ministry's goals if we are to get many people involved. Demonstrate how even small donations can make a significant difference in achieving the mission.

Use different fundraising strategies and methods such as online crowd funding, events, partnerships or grant writing to diversify the ministry's income sources.

So let each one give as he purposes in his heart, not grudgingly or of necessity; for God loves a cheerful giver.
2 Corinthians 9:7

#3 We must make an impact in ministry

Making a difference in ministry can be incredibly fulfilling, because giving our time, using our talents well and managing our resources wisely can have a significant impact over time. Because time represents our commitment to the work, talent embodies the unique skills and abilities we have or use to fulfil our responsibilities, while treasure represents the financial resources contributed to support the mission and work of the ministry.

When all three are harmoniously aligned, they form a holistic approach to serving God and others, fostering a community of love, support and spiritual growth that enables the ministry to thrive and make a meaningful impact.

> *And above all things have fervent love for one another, for "love will cover a multitude of sins." Be hospitable to one another without grumbling. As each one has received a gift, minister it to one another, as good stewards of the manifold grace of God. If anyone speaks, let him speak as the oracles of God. If anyone ministers, let him do it as with the ability which God supplies, that in all things God may be glorified through Jesus Christ, to whom belong*

the glory and the dominion forever and ever. Amen.

1 Peter 4:8-11

Let's see some ways that can lead us to make an impact in ministry:

1. Leading by Example

Leading by example in ministry means embodying the values, teachings and principles of our faith through our actions and behaviour; it means living in accordance with the beliefs and morals we preach, demonstrating humility, compassion, integrity and service to others.

In essence, it's about practising what we preach and being an example for others to follow in the pursuit of spiritual growth and a deeper connection with our faith.

Let your light so shine before men, that they may see your good works and glorify your Father in heaven.

Matthew 5:16

> *Let no one despise your youth, but be an example to the believers in word, in conduct, in love, in spirit, in faith, in purity.*
> **1Timothy 4:12**

2. Faithful Dedication

Faithful dedication involves an unwavering commitment and loyalty to a cause, belief or practice. It implies unwavering devotion, reliability and consistent effort towards a particular goal or purpose.

In the context of ministry, faithful dedication often involves a deep commitment to serve others, to follow teachings, and to live by principles with sincerity and consistency, even in the face of difficulties or challenges. It embodies a deep sense of loyalty and wholehearted devotion to one's beliefs or responsibilities.

Till I come, give attention to reading, to exhortation, to doctrine. Do not neglect the gift that is in you, which was given to you by prophecy with the laying on of the hands of the eldership. Meditate on these things; give yourself entirely to them, that your progress may be evident to all. Take heed to yourself and to the doctrine. Continue in them, for in doing this you will save both yourself and those who hear you.

1Timothy 4:13-16

Therefore, my beloved brethren, be steadfast, immovable, always abounding in the work of the Lord, knowing that your labour is not in vain in the Lord.

1 Corinthians 15:58

Chapter 6

SUSTAINING A LIFESTYLE OF MINISTRY

Sustaining a lifestyle of ministry is about maintaining a balance between serving others through our calling or vocation and caring for our personal well-being and growth. It's about maintaining a sustainable and fulfilling way of life that allows us to continue our ministry effectively while taking care of ourselves.

Maintaining a healthy and balanced life enables us to serve others more effectively. When we're emotionally, physically and spiritually well, our ability to support and guide those we serve is greatly enhanced. Given the emotional and mental demands of ministry, neglecting self-care can lead to burnout, hindering our ability to serve and causing personal distress.

A sustainable lifestyle ensures the long-term continuity and impact of our ministry. It breaks the cycle of intense periods followed by burnout and promotes more consistent and sustainable ministry.

> *Beloved, I pray that you may prosper in all things and be in health, just as your soul prospers.*
>
> **3 John 1:2**

#1 Maintaining a long-term commitment to ministry

Long-term commitment is essential for deeper relationships and understanding within the community we serve. It allows us to witness and be part of the lasting impact that consistent engagement can bring.

Consistency and longevity build trust. People often rely on stable, committed individuals in their times of need. Our steadfastness can become a source of strength and stability for those we serve.

1. Self-Care and Well-being

Self-care and wellbeing in ministry are essential for a balanced life. Making time for ourselves, engaging in activities we enjoy, maintaining healthy habits and nurturing positive relationships can make a significant contribution to our overall wellbeing.

It is important to know that we as Christians we belong to Christ both physically and spiritually; so taking care of ourselves is very important because our bodies are temples of the Lord and by doing so we are demonstrate that we love and honour God.

Or do you not know that your body is the temple of the Holy Spirit who is in you, whom you have from God, and you are not your own? For you were bought at a price; therefore glorify God in your body and in your spirit, which are God's.

1 Corinthians 6:19-20

For bodily exercise profits a little, but godliness is profitable for all things, having promise of the life that now is and of that which is to come.

1Timothy 4:8

2. Steadfastness and Trust in God

Perseverance and trust in God can serve as a foundation for sustaining a long-term commitment to ministry. By relying on faith, individuals can find the strength to persevere through challenges, remain committed to their calling and maintain a sense of purpose in the face of obstacles. It can also deepen their connection with their faith, guiding their actions and decisions as they serve God.

Consistency and longevity build trust. People often rely on stable, committed people in their times of need. Our steadfastness can become a source of strength and stability for those we minister to.

> *For you have need of endurance, so that after you have done the will of God, you may receive the promise*
>
> **Hebrew 10:36**

> *You will keep him in perfect peace, Whose mind is stayed on You, Because he trusts in You. Trust in the LORD forever, For in YAH, the LORD, is everlasting strength.*
>
> **Isaiah 26:3-4**

3. Avoiding Burnout

Avoiding burnout in ministry is crucial to maintaining our well-being and effectiveness in serving God and others. We also need to know that preventing burnout is an ongoing process that requires self-awareness and consistent effort. Prioritising our wellbeing enables us to serve God and others effectively and sustainably in our ministry.

We are encouraged to give our hearts and minds to the work of ministry without forgetting to take care of ourselves; for ministry requires good health. We need to set limits on our time and commitments to avoid being overwhelmed and to maintain a healthy work-life balance.

"Come to Me, all you who labour and are heavy laden, and I will give you rest. "Take My yoke upon you and learn from Me, for I am gentle and lowly in heart, and you will find rest for your

souls. "For My yoke is easy and My burden is light."
Matthew 11:28-30

#2 Strategies for maintaining a healthy lifestyle in ministry

As believers, we need to understand that good health is very important if we are to have a long-term ministry life and make a generational impact.

Finding a balance between physical, mental and spiritual well-being is part of maintaining a healthy lifestyle in ministry.

So teach us to number our days, That we may gain a heart of wisdom.
Psalms 90:12

1. Balanced Schedule

If we are to have a balanced schedule in our ministry, we need to prioritise tasks, make time for personal routines and regular exercise to boost energy and reduce stress, and set healthy boundaries between our work and personal lives to avoid over-commitment and exhaustion.

Above all, we need to get enough rest to rejuvenate our bodies and minds. A good night's sleep is essential for overall wellbeing. And never neglect our health; schedule regular check-ups with healthcare professionals to monitor our health status.

TO everything there is a season, A time for every purpose under heaven: A time to be born, And a time to die; A time to plant, And a time to pluck what is planted; A time to kill, And a time to heal; A time to break down, And a time to build up; A time to weep, And a time to laugh; A time to mourn, And a time to dance; A time to cast away stones, And a time to gather stones; A time to embrace, And a time to refrain from embracing; A time to gain, And a time to lose; A time to keep, And a time to throw away; A time to tear, And a time to sew; A time to keep silence, And a time to speak; A time to love, And a time to hate; A time of war, And a time of peace.

Ecclesiastes 3:1-8

2. Self-Reflection and Adaptability

Require it to regularly reflect on our lifestyle choices and make adjustments as necessary; be adaptable and open to change as circumstances dictate. Learn to delegate tasks and say no when necessary to avoid over-commitment.

Prioritise regular prayer and meditation on the Word of God for strength and guidance. If we want to stay spiritually engaged and motivated, we should develop our personal and professional lives through learning; build good relationships within our community or congregation, as social interaction can contribute positively to mental and emotional health.

Search me, O God, and know my heart; Try me, and know my anxieties; And see if there is any wicked way in me, And lead me in the way everlasting.

Psalms 139:23-24

Trust in the LORD with all your heart, And lean not on your own understanding; In all your ways acknowledge Him, And He shall direct your paths.

Proverbs 3:5-6

This should be our prayer as we ask God to lead us in His ways for His glory. Trusting in God is a conscious dependence on Him, much like relying on a tree for support. The command to know God means to observe Him and get to know Him in the process of living. These are the vital elements of faith that should fill every area of our lives.

#3 Guidance on fostering a culture of ministry within communities

Fostering a culture of ministry within communities is a noble endeavour that involves cultivating an environment where service, compassion and support thrive. It's about fostering a collective mindset that prioritises helping others, spreading kindness and meeting the needs of those within and beyond the community's boundaries. Creating such a culture requires intentional action, shared values, and a commitment to empowering individuals to serve and make a positive impact in their communities. Here are some steps you can take to foster such a culture:

1. **Leadership Example**
   Leaders should embody the values of service and inclusiveness and set the tone for others to follow.

Good leadership is about protecting, guiding, modelling and serving those you lead. But a good leader is not only one who serves his people, but also one who leads them to maturity.

Christian leaders must emulate the good examples of leadership by serving their followers well and teaching them the values of the kingdom of God. Jesus does not ask anyone to do what he is not willing to do. He came into this world as the Son of God, yet he did not have the normal attributes and advantages of a leader.

"just as the Son of Man did not come to be served, but to serve, and to give His life a ransom for many."
Matthew 20:28

2. **Clear Vision**
   Establish a clear vision and purpose for the ministry, communicating its goals and how it fits with the needs of the community.

Having a clear vision and purpose is crucial because it helps to identify the core principles that guide the ministry. These could be spiritual, ethical or social values that form the basis of the ministry's actions. Without God's revelation, people are lost.

Where there is no vision [no revelation of God and His word], the people are unrestrained
Proverbs 29:18 (Amplified)

3. **Collaboration**
   Encourage collaboration and teamwork between members to

create a more cohesive and supportive environment.

Throughout this section there is an emphasis on the obvious benefits of working together. The intimacy and sharing of life alleviates the problem of isolation and loneliness. A companion can provide support, comfort and protection in the work of ministry.

Two are better than one, because they have a good reward for their labour. For if they fall, one will lift up his companion. But woe to him who is alone when he falls, for he has no one to help him up

Ecclesiastes 4:9-10

CONCLUSION

This comprehensive examination of ministry culminates in an emphasis on the integral relationship between time, talent and treasure. The book stresses the importance of understanding the core of ministry, emphasising its roots in selfless service, leadership and compassion. Time is identified as a key element, urging individuals to manage their schedules skilfully, maintaining a balance between personal life and ministry commitments while optimising productivity.

In addition, the cultivation and effective use of talent plays a key role in the success of a thriving ministry. Fostering an environment that encourages individuals to contribute their unique skills helps to develop a dynamic and diverse community, ultimately increasing overall impact. In addition, stewardship - the prudent management of resources, whether financial, physical or human - is essential to the sustainable growth and achievement of ministry goals.

Addressing challenges and overcoming barriers is essential in the context of ministry, where conflict, burnout and resource constraints are common hurdles. The book offers strategic approaches to building resilience, resolving conflict and problem-solving effectively, thereby cultivating a more resilient and adaptable ministry culture.

Finally, the book advocates a lifestyle that embodies the principles of ministry. It goes beyond simply fulfilling assigned roles and emphasises the importance of living with an attitude of service, commitment and compassion. This approach ensures an ongoing and effective presence in communities.

Finally, the book emphasises that ministry is a comprehensive endeavour, encompassing multiple dimensions that emphasise the importance of unity, purposeful action and sustained commitment to serving others. Its aim is to equip individuals with the tools and insights they need not only to participate in ministry, but also to thrive and make a lasting, positive impact in their communities.

ABOUT THE AUTHOR

Elliot Luabeya Misamu is a servant of God at Centre Évangélique Missionnaire Rouah in Kinshasa, Democratic Republic of the Congo, and currently works as an associate Pastor at Gates of Zion Community in Accra, Ghana.

Elliot is a distinguished writer, preacher, and teacher of the Word of God. With a profound commitment to simplicity and clarity, he passionately shares the Word of God as presented within the pages of the Bible.

He holds a degree in theology from the Bible and Theological Institute of the Assemblies of God in Kinshasa, Democratic Republic of the Congo, and has obtained a certificate in pastoral and ministerial training from the Anagkazo Bible & Ministry Training Center in Mampong, Ghana. Furthermore, he has earned an executive diploma in theology from the Successful Ministers Academy in Accra, Ghana and a master's degree in systematic theology from the same institution.

REFERENCES AND SOURCES

[1] Dag Heward-Mills, The art of ministry: a handbook of practical ministry (Parchment house 2014)

[2] David Horton, The portable Seminary a master's level overview in one volume, second edition (Bethany House)

[3] Oxford English Dictionary second edition (1989)

[4] The Apologetic study of the bible, Holman Bible Publishers 2007 Nashville, Tennessee Pages 5401.

[5] Dr. Philip Aryee, Building relevant and impactful ministry (Destined to succeed publishers 2021)

6   Dr. Philip Aryee, Excellence in Ministry (Destined to succeed publishers 2021)

7   Dag Heward-Mills, Ministerial Ethics, second edition (Parchment house 2017)

8 Dag Heward-Mills, How you can make full proof of your ministry, (Parchment house 2017)

9 Dag Heward-Mills, Amplify your ministry with miracles and manifestations of the Holy Spirt, (Parchment house 2017)

10 The Expositor's Study Bible (Jimmy Swaggart ministry 2013)

11 Africa bible commentaries

12 The Amplified study bible